- Life Hacks Books –

Easy-to-read books to do better and feel better

SAVE TIME &
GET THINGS DONE

A 30-minute Life Hacks book on how to
increase your motivation,
be more productive,
more efficient,
get stuff done,
and save time for yourself.

The 30' Series – Vol. 1

SAVE TIME & GET THINGS DONE

If you are reading this book, chances are that you are somehow unhappy with the way your life goes at the moment. In fact, chances are that your daily work routine is part of the problem.

As you will find out, the main idea of this book is that being more productive and more efficient is NOT about doing more work. To the very opposite, being more efficient and more productive is about reaching similar results with fewer efforts, to save you time to do other things of your liking.

So, this book will give you some tips on how to re-balance your routine to free some time for yourself. It will give you an opportunity to think about why you want to be more productive and about what you intend to do with your extra time. It will help you put your finger on what is important for you and, ultimately, will help you identify and reinforce your motivation so that your efforts yield the greatest results possible over time.

ABOUT 'THE 30' SERIES'.

The Life Hacks Books are written with the aim of solving important problems that every single person faces one day or another, sooner or later. Only, most people do not seek to address those problems. You're apparently on the way to solving one problem, congratulations!

This book aims at giving you simple solutions and action plans that can be used immediately, after a quick and productive read. The rest will be for you to do. Take action now!

* * * *

IN THIS BOOK

CHALLENGE 1: PRODUCTIVITY IS NOT QUANTITY 7

CHALLENGE 2: YOU NEED A LONG-TERM PLAN 11

CHALLENGE 3: SET UP THOSE GOALS! 19

CHALLENGE 4: RE-CONSIDER YOUR WORKING METHODS & FIX YOUR DAILY ROUTINE.............23

CHALLENGE 5: THE PARETO OPTIMUM RULE...31

CHALLENGE 6: PROCRASTINATION AND MULTITASKING 35

CHALLENGE 7: STICK WITH REALISTIC AMBITIONS AND STAY POSITIVE!............................41

TAKE ACTION!..45

CHALLENGE 1: PRODUCTIVITY IS NOT QUANTITY

The very first challenge people face when they look for opportunities and solutions to become more efficient is to realize that productivity should not be about quantity.

Right, let me stop here and explore.

I know what you're thinking right now. There are two types of jobs: jobs that consist in producing quantity (pieces of equipment, cars, fast food, etc.), and jobs that only consist in producing quality (office work, marketing, design, etc.).

Those who work in a factory or behind a fast food counter and those how must observe quotas in their daily routine will say that efficiency for them is about producing more. I say this is not correct. There is a simple reason for that: even chain production requires quality. Making burgers is about quantity, but it is about quality in the first place and the same goes for building a car or producing thousands of tiny little screws.

If you are reading this book, chances are that you are not looking for a way to do more things every day. To be honest, my bet is that you are actually looking for a way to do things better, smarter, faster, so that you can save time to do other things you like. Right?

There you go. Being efficient or productive is not about doing a lot of things fast. And being more efficient and more productive is not about doing more things faster either!

Being more efficient is about getting the necessary amount of things done in a way that matches your work goals while preserving (and improving) your work / life balance. In other words, the stakes are very clear: efficiency is about doing the most of your time so as to achieve satisfying results with fewer efforts. Or, as they say, more is less.

Now, how do you do?

How do you see productivity?

Has productivity been about quantity for you so far?

Is getting things done about doing more?

What are you trying to achieve? What are you goals?

CHALLENGE 2: YOU NEED A LONG-TERM PLAN

Now that we've addressed the challenge of clarifying what efficiency and productivity mean, the second major challenge that most people face is to establish their own efficiency thresholds and targets.

Let's take a minute, I have a couple of questions for you. Take a pen, something to write on, and try to answer those questions honestly. It's important.

Are you happy with your work life / personal life balance?

Are you trying to be more efficient to make your

boss happy or are you trying to make more time for yourself?

Actually, do you have enough time for yourself?

What would you do with more time? Would you work more and stack more workload into your free time? Or would you use that extra time for more satisfying occupations? Which ones?

What I'm saying here is, the key to being more efficient is to know why you want to be more efficient and to have a long-term plan that will allow you to strategize, nurture and preserve your motivation along the way.

Decide what you want to achieve.

The foundation of a strong long-term plan is your motivation. You need to decide what you want to achieve in order to become more efficient at what you do, it's as simple as that!

Now, let me ask more questions, hopefully they will help you find your way.

If you are working for someone, there are three main reasons that most likely push you to want to be more efficient and productive.

One, you are trying to prove something to someone. There is nothing wrong with that, every single person with a boss does their best to demonstrate that they are the best suited to fill the role, that they are the hardest worker around, that they deserve the biggest race. Bla, bla bla, you get my point. If you fit in this category, your motivation could be a problem because in working to impress someone we end-up taking risks. You see your hard work as an effort and expect something in return, but your boss expects the best from you in exchange for your salary. In other words, if your hard work does not yield the benefits you expect, your motivation will be hit and your future work will suffer from it. Beware of this type of motivation.

Two, you are trying to be more efficient to save some time for yourself. You perhaps have too much work already, or you perhaps want to reduce your workload and release some pressure. In this case, your motivation is to improve your work style, your lifestyle and, most likely, your work/life balance. This type of motivation is strong, but it might not be strong enough to effectively keep you focused and determined. For example? Well, if your motivation is merely to go back home earlier every evening, chances are that you will progressively allow for procrastination and longer breaks to take over, because five minutes here and ten minutes there won't matter that much...

Three, you are trying to be more efficient to save time for yourself and get extra time to conduct some personal projects. For instance, to create a business in parallel to your job, to have some time to train for a marathon (good luck about that, I'll have some pizzas for moral support), to plan for a trip or to free some time to become a basketball coach at your kids' school. In this case, your motivation is not to improve your work style, it is to make the most of your time and live a passion. This type of motivation is very strong, because it actually gives you a real, practical and concrete reason to make an effort and work on yourself. Find your own goal and start from there.

Those who work for themselves usually have very strong motivations and very solid reasons to gain in efficiency.

First, time is money therefore being more efficient and more productive may yield more benefits, especially from a financial point of view.

Second, those who work for themselves may also do so to gain in freedom. When that's the case, gaining in efficiency and productivity becomes a matter of optimizing one's time, so as to obtain the same benefits while working less. Again, less is more.

Start from who you are and stick with it.

All this means that the first thing when it comes to becoming more efficient and more productive is to find a strong motivation for doing so. Your motivation will get you there, so find it, write it down, and stick with it.

Another element you need to stick with is who you are. That means, your values, your beliefs, the way you want to live your life.

As long as you are clear with what you are trying to achieve and as long as your project is in line with who you are, you will be able to stand for your project and you will gain extra strength and motivation to be more efficient and more productive.

Let's reformulate, just in case. Your quest for greater efficiency must come from yourself and must be about yourself. You are the only one at best to create success targets, and you are the only one capable of assessing whether you are indeed succeeding (or not) with your project. Do not overestimate your abilities, of course, but do not worry about what the others say either. This must be about you.

Now, how do you do?

What are your motivations?

Why do you want to be more efficient?

What does efficiency mean to you?

What are the "things" you need to do?

Are you trying to achieve more for someone else or for yourself?

Is it about proving something?

Is it about making time for other projects?

CHALLENGE 3: SET UP THOSE GOALS!

The next step is to define your goals and write them down (so you can come back to them occasionally). Now, there are two complementary methods for setting your goals.

SMART goals, and the Big black rocks & sand methods. We are going to look at both.

SMART goals

The first method consists in defining 'S.M.A.R.T goals' that are Specific, Measurable, Attainable, Realistic and Timely.

Specific means precise. Your goals cannot be broad. 'I want more time, I'll see later what I can do with it' is not precise but 'I want to save enough time to have my Fridays off' is precise.

Measurable means easy to assess. Saying that you want your Fridays off means that you can assess very easily and regularly if you are achieving your goal or not. How many Fridays off have you managed to enjoy recently?

Attainable and realistic means that you must go for something that you know you can achieve. Having your Fridays off is attainable, but having your Wednesdays and Thursdays off too is not realistic. Not right now, anyway.

Timely is another level of measurability. How long are you giving yourself to reach your goal?

Big black rocks and sand

Once your SMART goals are set, try the big black rocks and sand method.

Imagine a long but narrow vase. Now, imagine your SMART goals as big black rocks that you place inside the vase one after another so they pile-up.

But before putting another black rock in the vase, think about it carefully.

What is that goal about? Is it precise? Can I follow-up on it? Is it a fantasy or can I action that goal and really make it a reality? Do I need more time to work on it and make it clearer? Should I keep it for later? The rocks are your priorities.

Once the priorities are set, pour some sand inside the vase and fill the gaps. The sand illustrates the non-priorities, those tiny little things that get in the way and fill the gaps, those things that will consume your time and hide your priorities progressively.

Simply put? Set up your goals and stick with them.

Think!

Let me insist. Setting goals requires serious thinking and planning.

In order to work on being more efficient, you need to be clear about what you are going to achieve. I said 'going to achieve', not 'going to try to achieve'.

So, you need to think and brainstorm. Alone works, but having a serious discussion with someone close makes a lot of sense too. What you want here is to make a selection of the sharpest and more relevant ideas.

Another way to back your thinking is to try backwards planning. In plain English, since your SMART goal has a timely aspect (the T), you can start from the expectation deadline you determined and work backwards in order to plan what steps will have to be put into place in order to achieve results on time.

Now, how do you do?

How could you adapt the SMART goal system to your own motivations?

What does the Big black rocks method tell you?

Have you ever thought about asking someone's opinion on your projects? Could brainstorming help setting your own goals?

CHALLENGE 4: RE-CONSIDER YOUR WORKING METHODS & FIX YOUR DAILY ROUTINE

Now that your goals are set, you can start working on being more efficient. In case I didn't make myself very clear, the preparation phase is more than half the work, the rest is only implementation. Make sure you get that step right, or you will lose time and won't be efficient!

Make time for yourself!

A great way to be more efficient is to make time for yourself in your own agenda. Again, less is more and being more efficient is about achieving similar or better results with fewer work involved, right? So, preserving time for yourself is the basis.

If you work for someone and have a boss, try to negotiate that Friday off twice a month, and then work on your productivity to compensate and still achieve results.

If you work for yourself and have some freedom in the way you plan your time, keep some slots off on your diary to make sure that time will be yours to play with. If you asked, I would for instance say that I keep my Fridays off to do some reading and some writing...

Now that you have inserted that big rock in your vase, add another one and a third one. On your diary, the rocks would materialize as big chunks of time that you keep for progressing on your work, without interruption. For instance, Monday morning is for administrative things, Monday lunch time is for meeting clients, Monday afternoon is for meetings, Tuesday and Wednesday are for research or business development (depending on what you do, obviously) and Thursday is to be kept for ... your decision to make!

Set-up or Fix your Daily Routine

The next challenge is to set-up or fix your daily routine. As a reminder, the first step to more efficiency is to plan some time for yourself because the very idea of increasing your productivity is to save time for yourself.

In line with the previous section, without a surprise, the idea is to plan for your daily routine. Is there a day you want to keep for yourself? Plan for it! Is there a specific day that needs to be kept for meeting clients? Plan for it! Are there any new projects to be included in your work pipeline? Plan for that too. But remember, being more efficient is not about creating yourself more work...

Now, here is a list of ideas that you can use to make the most of your time.

Plan some time for yourself early in the morning or late at night. I like writing at night because I live in a big building with a city view that I find inspiring when all is calm out there, but some would rather have a writing, reading, running or meditating routine first thing in the morning to start the day their way. Do you take time for yourself every day?

Just start, go on! For many people, the hardest part is the beginning. Writers call it the page block, others simply don't manage to get into their work because their mind is busy elsewhere. To gain in efficiency, boost yourself, decide, and start. Do it, that's it.

This implies finding the proper environment where you will be able to work. In my case for instance, my office is always very quiet. This doesn't work for me. Of course, some silence is important sometimes, but activity is also good for stimulation so I regularly work out of my office, in cafes and public place, to gain in productivity. What is your perfect environment?

Take a two-minute break here and then. I'm not talking about a coffee break here. I'm talking about taking two minutes to stop what you're doing, on your way to work or between two chunks of uninterrupted work to either enjoy a sunrise or empty your mind and refocus. This is a simple, little and inexpensive reward, you'd be stupid not to enjoy it, right? So, again, stop, breathe, then move on.

To-do lists and checklists are precious tools when it comes to increasing your efficiency. One, they helping making sure that you don't forget something. Second, if used pragmatically and strategically, they can help you think about the big picture and will help you avoid doing and re-doing things just because preparation was insufficient. Again, be precise and write clear goals on your list. In my case, for instance, an uninterrupted block of work would not be about writing, it would be about writing a 3000 words chapter or article. Precisely. Less is more, so plan for less and achieve more. Do you have a list? If not, put it on your to-do list...

Don't stay alone. Working on your efficiency does not mean staying alone. In fact, you should also plan time to discuss and exchange with other people on your work and projects. As far as your work is concerned, spending time to brainstorm every once in a while, is a great way to obtain feedback and make sure that you are going in the right direction. It is also a fantastic way to receive hints and clues on things you probably didn't think about, in which case the time you spend discussing will save you time later on. Include ideas as you go and you will avoid doing things all over again later.

Learn to say no! Not being alone does not mean letting others decide for you and in reality being efficient requires to learn how to say no! To be efficient at what you are supposed to do and to reach your personal goals, you need to focus. This means that you need to consider carefully each new potential commitment and refuse it if it doesn't serve you goals. You also need to avoid being interrupted, whether by unwanted meetings or by unwanted phone calls and emails. I'll come to that later.

Reflect. It is also very important to take time to think and reflect about how you are doing. From a work perspective, reflecting means analyzing how your work works. Have you made sure that you are going in the right direction? Are you doing it regularly? Have you involved anyone in the project to obtain some feedback and confirm that you are in the right direction?

The idea of thinking out of the box is also very important. My way of thinking is based on getting the big picture. I need to make sure that I have a correct overview of the projects I manage before going into the details. That requires doing a little bit of digging in the first place, but it is a real time saver in the end because it avoids missing important points and avoids moving backwards.

The idea of thinking laterally is very much similar to this. Instead of thinking about who can decide for you, think about the alternatives and include them in your program. Being able to propose instead of merely waiting for someone's decision will make you much more efficient! You will save time because you won't need to wait for someone, and you will keep control over what you do which will help a lot with your working autonomy. Less is more!

Reflecting is also about measuring the progresses you make on your personal development goals. It of course depends on how much freedom you have in your daily routine (especially if you do have a boss), but the idea here is to make sure that your work schedule does match your personal goals. Of course! Because less is more, try to think about how you are actually doing. Is your program working as planned? Can you improve? What do you need to adapt? What unexpected developments have you faced? What are the impacts on your long-term needs?

Now, how do you do?

Does your daily routine allow you to get things done?

To get the right things done? The things you want to do?

Do you allow time in your routine to do what matters most without being disturbed?

Time for yourself perhaps?

How about re-thinking your routine just now?

To what extent could lists help?

Can you say no? Would that help with your priorities?

CHALLENGE 5: THE PARETO OPTIMUM RULE

I'm sure you've heard of the Pareto rule: 20% of the work you do must yield 80% of your results.

In other words, all your daily routine must focus on achieving 80% of results with the least amount of work possible. Start with the boring and unpleasant work that needs to be done, or give it away to someone who will do it for you. Then your day will focus on the constructive stuff. And without much surprise, the constructive stuff is... the big rocks in the vase!

At the end of each day or first thing in the morning, make sure that your day will be about doing the most important tasks! If you can achieve more, do it, but if your goal has been achieved then you have been efficient and that is more than enough. Less is more, remember?

Stick with the uninterrupted chunks of work mentioned previously. If you have organized your week to save time for you, you have most likely also followed my advice regarding the importance of planning for concentration blocks. The idea here is that by focusing on specific tasks without distraction you will see major progress take place. No interruption means results, results mean satisfaction, satisfaction means efficiency. Period.

Now, how do you determine which activity is to be considered a 20% important activity that will deliver on 80% of your goals? You need to identify your priorities depending on two criteria: importance and urgency.

Warning: this bit is very important, read it twice.

Focus on the important but not urgent. This way, you plan ahead, avoid having to deal with important and urgent issues and never feel like someone is holding a knife under your throat.

This then leaves you with non-important but urgent matters (on which you can decide, or not) while anything that is not important and not urgent is not worth spending time on. *Read that again.*

Now, reflect on this and reconsider your list of urgent and important jobs so you can deal with them in due time and be efficient.

Now, how do you do?

Do you sometimes make sure that your day will be about doing your most important tasks?

What are the 20% activities you need to focus on?

What is important for you? What is urgent? Should you focus on important or urgent?

How can you set and organize your priorities then

CHALLENGE 6: PROCRASTINATION AND MULTITASKING

Procrastination and multitasking are trendy words but they can be terrible for whatever you have. All is not black or white, however. What matters is how you plan your work.

Procrastination is not necessarily about wasting your time

Procrastination is the art of doing tomorrow something you could not right now if you actually wanted to. But doing just that is not necessarily a bad thing, especially if you know what you are doing.

Some will tell you – motivational articles on the internet do this a lot - that taking more time will not help you make better decisions. The longer the decision, in fact, the greater the concerns and the smaller the chances of actually making a decision.

But this might actually be terrible advice, because there are different ways of seeing procrastination. One relates to decision-making, the other relates to creativity.

The most important thing when it comes to making decisions is the ability to think, balance and mitigate pros and cons, or risks. But in this case the delay is not about wasting time, it is about taking the time to actually think!

To this extent, procrastination is not only about delaying, it is about taking some time to let new ideas come to you. Whilst you focus on one issue, your mind will wander and make progress on other things. If you allow yourself a little bit of that, the chances of seeing things from new angles will be stronger than if you just rush-in. By the same token, you might therefore achieve more results. As once said by a distinguished

TED speaker, 'you call it procrastination, I call it thinking'.

Hence, the important thing when it comes to being more efficient and productive is to make sure that you do take the necessary time to think and reflect, providing however that you do not use that time as an excuse. You're right, that sounds very obvious, but chances are that you've used the excuse card a lot already, right?

Procrastination is the art of getting nothing done unless you do it with a purpose. When it comes to making decisions, do not rush-in. Give yourself a delay and decide.

Multitasking is a myth

My wife often teases me because she says I can only do one thing at the time while she, as most women, can obviously multitask. I know you are smiling right now. Probably for a different reason depending on whether you are a man or a woman, but you know I'm right.

So, let's be clear, multitasking is a myth, and it is the best way to do nothing at all. To be efficient, you need to focus on uninterrupted chunks of work and stick with them. Focus, work, progress.

To avoid interruptions, you need to build up a firewall around you. There are various methods for doing this.

One is to learn how to say no, another is to switch your phone off (the notifications, at least).

A third solution is to refrain from looking at your emails all day. I am extremely serious here, this point is a cheap but extremely efficient life changer! First, giving people immediate answers suggests that you are indeed available anytime. Instead, teach your contacts the idea that you will get back to them in due time. Second, reading and answering emails here and then is the best way to do nothing with your time because you will not be able to switch rapidly enough from one task to another. Just check them twice a day at best, and progressively move down to emails once a day. You will gain in productivity.

A fourth solution is to stay away from social networks as much as possible. Social networks are about interaction by nature, therefore any minute you are about to spend on social networks will be an opportunity for you to socialize and it will cost you time. Badly used time. Keep these for later, never mix social networks with work, or you will kill your efficiency goals in a breeze.

Now, how do you do?

Honestly, how often do you procrastinate?

Why do you procrastinate? Do you lack interest for what you have to do?

Have you ever thought of procrastination as a way to take some creativity times, whilst working on something else?

Would you be able to focus more if you had different priorities?

Are you a multitasker?

Can you do everything well?

Could reviewing your methods and refocusing on specific tasks help you achieve results faster?

CHALLENGE 7: STICK WITH REALISTIC AMBITIONS AND STAY POSITIVE!

The last challenge is to stick with realistic ambitions, to keep learning and reflecting, and to celebrate your achievements.

Perfection does not exist.

As explained before, efficiency depends on your ability to set up Attainable and Realistic goals that can be Measured. So stick with realistic ambitions and don't try to reach perfection because you will never reach it.

At best, you will do things over and over. At worst, you will discourage yourself and will never start implementing your projects. Stick with ambitions on which you can deliver, and celebrate to boost your motivation.

Being positive is important for productivity.

Those who complain all the time rarely achieve anything because all they see is obstacles and limits.

The positive ones, in contrast, see opportunities and solutions. Hence, condition yourself and your humor will impact your efficiency!

Reflect and learn to move forward (sometimes).

Right, you should never give-up on your projects but you can leave aside some options that do not work. Conducting a project is an investment and sometimes investors have no choice but to move on, therefore accepting to face some irretrievable 'sunk costs'.

So, admitting failure and moving on is an

important aspect of being positive. It helps limiting the losses and therefore limits negative impacts on efficiency.

Celebrate and repeat.

Celebrating and repeating the process are the best ways of being positive for two reasons.

One, celebrating is about rewarding your work therefore it will give you the confirmation that your efficiency efforts have paid.

Two, repeating the process will improve your efficiency even more because it will give you an opportunity to validate your learning while, unsurprisingly, giving you another chance to be even more efficient.

Now, how do you do?

How realist are your ambitions and goals so far? Does this make sense?

Have you been trying to achieve perfection? Could this be counter-productive in the end?

What is the impact of mood on your results? Could positive-thinking and motivations help you achieve the results you hope to achieve?

.

TAKE ACTION!

Now, let's be very honest, this book will only help you save time and get things done if YOU actually do something for yourself. In other words, the next step is for you to take action! So, let me repeat the main point for you.

Being more productive is not about doing more, it is about achieving the same results in less time.

In order to be more productive, you need a long-term plan. Therefore, your main challenge will be to decide what you want to achieve. Start from who you are, find out why you need to save time for yourself, and stick with that.

Then, you need to write down your goals.

SMART goals that you will then be able to work on with my rock & sand strategy.

Once your strategy is set up and your goals are clearly established, the next step is to re-consider your working methods. This starts with preserving some time for yourself and fix your daily routine. Avoid staying alone, learn to say no and... reflect on your progress on a regular basis to adapt your life and work-style to your long-term goals.

Remember that when it comes to being more productive to save time for yourself, less is more. The 20/80 Pareto Optimum rule applies without a doubt: focus on the 20% of work that will yield 80% of your routine and long-term results.

Remember, also, that procrastination is bad for whatever you have, and that multitasking is a myth. My wife will mock me for saying that, but the reality is, you can only do one thing efficiently at the time. Pick what you need to do, do it, and move on.

Remember, finally, that perfection does not exist. Stick with realistic ambitions, stay positive, and reflect on you projects to adjust as you progress!

* * * *

If you found this book interesting, please consider giving it some stars on Amazon!

Thank you in advance!

* * * *

About The 30' Series.

The Life Hacks Books (and eBooks) are written with the aim of solving important problems that every single person faces one day or another, sooner or later. Only, most people do not seek to address those problems. You're apparently on the way to solving one problem, congratulations!

This book aims at giving you simple solutions and action plans that can be used immediately, after a quick and productive read. The rest will be for you to do. Take action now!

Life Hacks Books:

The 30' Series:

Volume 1: Get Thing Done!

Volume 2: Smarter? Yes, Smarter!

The Leadership Hacks Series:

Volume 1: If Steve Jobs was Coaching You.

ARE YOU INTERESTED IN LEADERSHIP?

FREE ABSTRACT:

LEADERSHIP DEVELOPMENT: IF STEVE JOBS WAS COACHING YOU

Charismatic Leadership Lessons Borrowed from Steve Jobs for High Potential People and Leaders.

The Leadership Hacks Series

Leadership Books to learn new things & feel smarter!

- Life Hacks Books –

Steve Jobs co-founded Apple in 1976 with Steve Wozniak. Both had the exceptional ambition to bring computers into every home. Forty years later, computers are indeed in every home, the Apple ones in particular, not to forget those we carry in our pockets, jackets or handbags on a daily and hourly basis.

But beyond this business success is a fascinating leadership story that numerous articles and comments have tried to analyze. In most of them, the question is always the same: whether or not Steve Jobs was a good leader and how he actually managed products, people and business developments throughout his career.

Still, one question remains unanswered for: how could things work for you if Steve Jobs was actually coaching *you*?

This book focuses on this exact question and provides a comprehensive review of the many skills and difficulties that have been characteristic of Steve Jobs' leadership.

More specifically, it analyzes ten of the major challenges faced by most entrepreneurs nowadays and offers about thirty-five leadership tips that can be borrowed from Jobs' life and experience to help the readers see through his leadership methods.

At the end of each session, of course, a series of questions is provided to help the readers think further and improve *their own leadership* by applying the discussions to their own management style. It's up to you now...

[...]

LEADERSHIP HACK #3:
LEAD AND INSPIRE

The third important pillar of Steve Jobs' leadership was his ability to lead and inspire, and he applied four important rules to his daily work. One was that you need to be the person in charge. A second rule was that setting goals is a priority. A third was that you need to develop an ability to inspire. A fourth was rule was about being persistent, always.

Be the captain, be in charge. Jobs was known for saying "Don't let the noise of others' opinions drown out your own inner voice". This quote can certainly be applied to the previously mentioned consumer-based approach to business development, but in reality, the idea here is to make sure that there is only one captain in the boat.

Leadership is about making decisions and, while consulting with others is important, only the captain decides what happens next. How many businesses fail routinely because the management team fails to make important decisions? Thousands! So, under Jobs' leadership, decisions only came from one person. Him!

The lesson here is: be the captain, be in charge of the vision, decide on the innovation and lead forward. Chances are, indeed, that while you might find this very logical, you are not really deciding alone in practice. Are you?

Setting goals on a regular basis is a key aspect of leadership. You might have a passion and a vision, but without goals there are no directions, no benchmarks and no way for you to organize a follow-up system!

Hence, Steve Jobs was very keen on setting up short-term and long-term goals alike. Hence, he could ensure that his strategy could evolve in time depending on his markets evolutions, depending on his users' needs and depending on his own beliefs, ideas and intuitions. In other words, long term goals give you the direction and a roadmap while short term goals give you means to implement the strategy.

To be reactive to market evolutions and to assess how well you are doing, you therefore need to set-up benchmarks and, obviously, short-term, medium-term and long-term goals. Think about it, we'll come back to this in a minute.

Remember that leading forward requires an ability to inspire others. Goals are not the only thing. While a common argument in business methods, courses and books will teach you how to be a seller, Steve Jobs rather believed in his ability to inspire others.

Of course, it is likely that – as mentioned before – most industry actors reviewed their models to follow Jobs' vision because they didn't have a choice at all.

Nonetheless, Jobs certainly did great at inspiring many, starting with his consumers. In turning his consumers into early adopters and eventually into inspired adepts, Jobs has progressively turned generations of consumers and entrepreneurs alike into followers! Many technologies and apps nowadays are driven by the Apple innovations, millions of businesses not only follow the lead but also made the revolution theirs, thus continuing Jobs' efforts and making is vision an absolute and unquestionable reality. Have you taken steps to try and inspire?

Persistence is another skill sharp leaders cannot live without. Think about it. What unique skill – apart from talent, vision, anticipation and inspiration – could take you from building a computer in a garage to building a worldwide community of users and followers while making you one of the major innovators and business leaders after being fired from your own company?

Persistence!

As a reminder, Steve Jobs not only persisted on creating the most innovative tools of our modern world. He also persisted in keeping Apple a striving company. Jobs created Apple in 1976 and was fired from it in 1985 by a CEO he nominated himself. Yet, he took over later and even had another company he built (NeXT) sold to Apple in 1997.

While this seems ironical, the one skill behind those developments was always persistence and the belief – or should I say conviction – that an idea was worth fighting for without limits.

Persistence, or the ability not to give up, is therefore a key aspect of Jobs' leadership and a skill that any leader must acquire and nurture. Of course, no one can prevent discouragement. But persistent people all have in common the ability to go past difficulties so as to make their vision a reality. In line with the 'one boat one captain' rule, persistence is about being able to stand for yourself, about making decisions that you, as a leader, deem visionary and fit.

Now, can *you* inspire?

Again, take a minute to think. How would you reply to these questions if Steve Jobs asked them as part of a face-to-face meeting?

Are you in charge? Are you really in charge? Do you take command when it comes to creating the vision and making it happen? Are you occasionally or regularly to leadership issues involving decision-making needs?

Do you set goals? Your own goals? Do you listen and take your teams' goals into account when setting yours? How about short-term, medium-term and long-term goals?

Can you inspire others? Have you even tried? What steps could you take tomorrow to lead others to follow you and support your undertakings? If you had to describe yourself, how inspiring would you be? Are you managing your team so as to achieve numbers and statistics or do you leave room for inspiring and meaningful leadership that allows your staff (and clients) to adhere to your vision, agree to it and make it theirs?

Are you persistent? People always have ideas, they start new ideas but usually give-up on them very fast. Are you persistent enough to see your ideas become a reality? Do you give-up easily? Are you easily discouraged? Have you considered persisting and insisting more because an idea is worth it?

LEADERSHIP DEVELOPMENT: IF STEVE JOBS WAS COACHING YOU

Charismatic Leadership Lessons Borrowed from Steve Jobs for High Potential People and Leaders.

– Life Hacks Books –

– The Leadership Series –

- Life Hacks Books –
Easy-to-read books to do better and feel better

58903946R00045

Made in the USA
Middletown, DE
22 December 2017